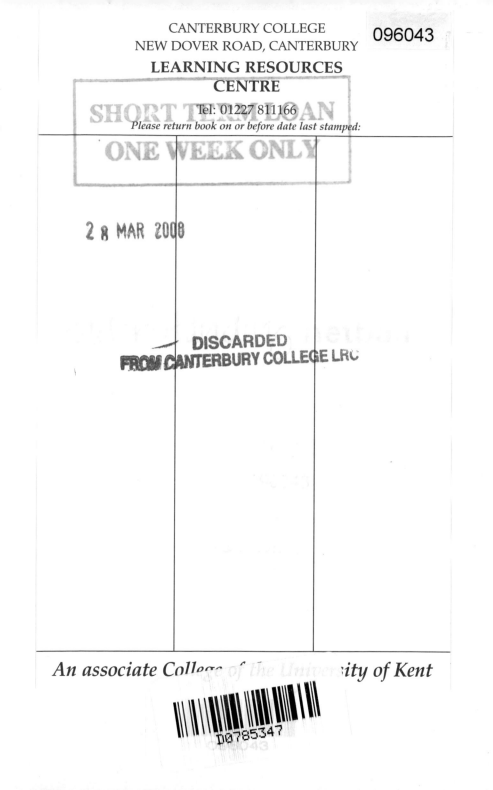

ISBN-13: 978-1-905540-12-9
ISBN-10: 1-905540-12-4

Author
Julia Hickey

Specialist Consultant
Anita Navin

With thanks to Glyn Sutcliffe (indexer)

Cover photo © Action Images

Throughout this publication, the use of pronouns he, she, him, her and so on are interchangeable and intended to be inclusive of both male and female netball players.

Published by

Coachwise 1st4sport

Coachwise 1st4sport
Chelsea Close
Off Amberley Road
Armley
Leeds LS12 4HP
Tel: 0113-231 1310 Fax: 0113-231 9606
Email: enquiries@1st4sport.com
Website: www.1st4sport.com

Produced and designed by Coachwise Business Solutions, a brand of Coachwise Ltd. If you wish to publish some material for your organisation, please contact us at enquiries@coachwisesolutions.co.uk

If you are an author and wish to submit a manuscript for publication, please contact us at enquiries@1st4sport.com

060071

Contents

Foreword

Netball is an exciting, fast and dynamic team game that has given me a great deal of pleasure since I started playing. *Understanding Netball* captures this nature of the sport and its emphasis on the competitive spirit ensures that it is a brilliant guide for those learning the sport, or even those who want to touch up on their knowledge of the game.

As there are also lots of rules in netball, the book's handy breakdown of the laws will help you get them right and be a better player! As well as keeping to the rules when you play, you need to learn the game's skills and then capitalise on these with other team members, so that you can pull together to achieve a common goal – to win! *Understanding Netball* really emphasises the need for skills and provides useful handy hints as to how to perform them; these are highlighted using clear and recognisable symbols, which make this a very reader-friendly resource to have. This book also provides fantastic Internet links for you to explore to find out more about our top players and how to get involved in the sport.

I enjoy netball for many reasons, but you do need dedication and must work hard to get to the top. I love to compete and, when you win in big competitions, it makes all the hard work worthwhile. By playing netball for England, I have also had the opportunity to travel a lot and see different countries, meet new people and make new friends; however, above all, I *love* to represent my country and I am very *proud* to do so.

So, if you want fun and enjoy a sport...read *Understanding Netball* and get out there and play netball!

Amanda Newton
Captain of the England Netball Team

Chapter 1
Getting the Most Out of *Understanding* Netball

There are three possible ways of reading this book. Whichever way you choose, have fun and enjoy the game of netball.

1 You can read the book from beginning to end.
   Most chapters are divided into three parts:

* The first part of the chapter provides information that will help you understand netball, whether you want to watch or play the game.
* The second part is a **summary** of key information about the netball laws dealt with in that chapter.
* The final part provides **training** tasks to help you check whether you have understood the rules and information covered in the chapter.

2 You can read just a chapter or a section of the book that you think might be useful to you.

* Scan through the book and look for the information (represented by icons) that interests you most. Here is a key to the icons.

	Training. Test your knowledge of the contents of each chapter.	**GK**	Netball skill. If you want to develop your netball skills further, you should join a local club or side where you will be given advice and coaching.
	Use the web. Follow the link to surf the net.	**?**	Questions and answers. Common questions about netball with clear explanations.

* Use the summary sections of each chapter to brush up on your understanding.
* Test your understanding by completing the training activities at the end of each chapter.

3 You can complete the following quiz to find out what aspects of the game you need to sharpen up on. Check the answers to see how well you did and to identify the chapters you should work on.

Quiz

1 A maximum number of seven
players from a team is allowed on
court during a match but how
many must be on court for the
game to start?
a 4.
b 5.
c 10.

2 How far away from a player with
the ball do defenders have to
stand?
a It's a contact sport, so there is no
set distance.
b 90 cm (0.9 m).
c 300 cm (3 m).

3 What are the different kinds of
passes that an umpire can award
against players when they infringe
the rules?
a Free passes and penalty passes.
b Direct free passes, indirect free
passes and penalty passes.
c The umpire does not award
passes, he awards goals against
the team that has infringed the
rule.

4 How many players from a team can
score goals?
a All of them.
a Three – the goal shooter (GS),
the goal attack (GA) and the wing
attack (WA).
a Two – the goal shooter (GS) and
the goal attack (GA).

5 How many sections is a netball
court divided into?
a 3 (thirds).
b 4 (quarters).
c 6 (sixths).

6 What is a shoulder pass?
a It is a one-handed throw designed
to pass the ball accurately over a
long distance.
b It is a defensive system for
keeping the ball out of reach of
the attacking team, by ensuring
that players keep their shoulders
turned away from the attackers.
c It is the prescribed method for
bringing a substitute onto the
court.

7 When are penalty passes awarded?
a A free pass is the only award that
can be given to a non-offending
team during a netball match.
b They are awarded for all footwork
infringements.
c They are awarded against teams
who break the obstruction and
contact rules.

Chapter 2
Netball Through the Ages

Netball was developed from basketball, which was invented in 1891 by Dr Naismith. It was introduced to a group of teachers who enjoyed the game and transported it across the country, and then across the world. Today, there are more than 55,000 registered netball participants in England alone.

Netball in the 19th Century

Key Dates

1895	Basketball was introduced to a group of female students at Madame Osterberg's Physical Training College in England. The first goal rings and nets were actually two waste-paper baskets, which did not have holes in the bottom! This meant that every time a goal was scored, one of the umpires had to climb a ladder to get the ball back. There were also several collisions, caused partially no doubt by the long skirts and impractical blouses worn by the female participants.
1897	Netball was played outdoors for the first time.
1898	The court was divided into thirds for the first time.

Netball in the 20th Century

Key Dates

1900	The official rules of netball were created and printed by the Ling Association (it is now the Physical Education Institution).
1924	New Zealand created a national netball association.
1926	England created a national netball association.
1927	Australia created a national netball association.
1938	National netball teams from Australia and New Zealand competed against one another for the first time.
1949	National netball teams from England, Scotland and Wales competed against each other for the first time.
1957	A conference about the international rules for netball was held, so that everyone would play by the same rules, no matter where they were in the world.
1960	The International Federation of Netball Associations (IFNA) was formed. An international code of play was introduced.

1963	The first World Championships were held in Eastbourne and the Australians emerged as winners. The championships have been held every four years since.
1984	The National Clubs League started.
1993	Netball was recognised by the Olympic Committee.
1998	Netball was included in the Commonwealth Games for the first time. The gold medal was won by Australia, with England collecting the bronze medal.

Profile

A son of Scottish immigrants, the Canadian-born **Dr James Naismith** (1861–1939) invented basketball in 1891 in Springfield, Massachusetts. He had been instructed by the head of his organisation (it later became the Young Men's Christian Association) to create an indoor game for a group of rowdy students, who had no release for their energies during the winter months. Naismith had just 14 days to create a game to occupy their attention. By the end of his two weeks, Naismith had written 13 rules that remain the bedrock of the modern game of basketball. He must have been amazed when basketball became an Olympic sport at the Berlin Games of 1936. Then, of course, there is netball – a game in its own right, developed as a result of one man, **Dr Toles**, who, during a visit to England, introduced the game to a group of female students.

Netball in the 1930s.

Netball in the 21st Century

Netball has gone from strength to strength. There are now more people than ever playing the game, including male competitors who have their own tournaments.

Find out more about the history of netball by visiting www.england-netball.co.uk/ membership/prodshow.cfm or by downloading this pdf: www.sportfocus.com/ pdf/History%20of%20Netball.pdf

Find out more about Dr James Naismith at www.hoophall.com /halloffamers/Naismith.htm

Chapter 3
Getting Started

An impromptu game of netball can take place anywhere – in the park, on the beach or in your back garden. The rules that make netball unique are the footwork rules, the defending rules and the fact that a player in possession of the ball has three seconds in which to pass it to another player.

 What sort of equipment do I need to buy if I want to start playing netball?

At first, to practise throwing and catching skills, you do not really need much more than a ball and a pair of trainers. Once you have joined a club or a team, you will need to buy a pair of specialist netball shoes. England Netball recommends that players buy Asics netball training shoes because they are lightweight, supportive, offer stability to protect ankles and have good grip. Once you have been playing netball for a while and have had an opportunity to find out your best position, you may wish to buy more specialised shoes. For example, defenders have extra reinforcement in their shoes to protect their feet when they are playing in the goal circle. If you join a local club or team and receive coaching, you will be able to get advice about the best kind of footwear to buy.

 How old do I have to be before I can start playing netball?

The England Netball Association has developed First Step Netball for 7–9-year-olds. There are only four players per side, the post is reduced in size, a smaller area of the court is used and the whole game lasts only 10 minutes. First Step Netball is a fun game, designed to develop some of those all-important ball

and evasion skills. High 5 Netball is designed for 9–11-year-olds and is a modified game that extends skills and teamwork, and emphasises the fun element of netball, with seven players per team, all of whom rotate positions. If you live in Wales, check out Dragon Netball and, in Scotland, Thistle Netball.

 Find out more about Dragon Netball by going to www.welshnetball.co.uk and selecting the 'Dragon Netball' button on the menu at the top of the page.

For information about Thistle Netball, visit www.netballscotland.com/thistlenetball.aspx and, if you're interested in High 5 Netball, go to the England Netball site at www.england-netball.co.uk and select 'the game' button from the menu at the top of the page. You should see 'High 5 Netball' listed on the next menu down the left-hand side of the page.

 Isn't netball a game just for girls?

No! Boys up to the age of 11 can play High 5. There is also a number of male teams that play against each another.

© Action Images

Player profile
Tracey Neville is the talented sister of Gary and Phil Neville, who are more famous for their footballing skills. With more than 70 England caps to her name since 1993, she has made a career as a goal attack (GA) and a wing attack (WA). She began her career playing for Bury, before moving to Northern Thunder. She helped England win bronze at the 1998 Commonwealth Games and also represented her country in 2002, when England's netball squad missed out on a medal. She has demonstrated her commitment to the England netball squad by her determination to overcome injury.

I want to play netball. Do I need a special diet and to be very fit?

A successful netball player needs to have flexibility and muscular endurance, as well as speed, agility, balance, fast reaction times, power, coordination and cardiovascular fitness. This means that, without a nutritional diet, the most talented netball player in the world will suffer as a result of the wrong kinds of food and drink being consumed.

If players consume the wrong food or drink on a regular basis, they will not be able to train as hard, nor play as long. This means that players need lots of carbohydrates to give them energy. Players also need to take care of their muscles, as there is always the risk of injury, so plenty of protein is also important. Carbohydrate, fat and protein are the three main fuels for exercise. How much of each should we consume? Well, that depends on the amount of exercise a player does. It is also important to eat the right kinds of food before and after a match. A post-match recovery snack might include pasta and chicken.

Players can also keep up their level of fitness by being careful about the amount of liquid they drink. Water and sports drinks are the best forms of fluid a netball player can take onboard during a match or training session. Try not to drink lots of fizzy, sugar-filled drinks. Remember that fluid is lost during matches and training as a result of sweating. If your mouth feels dry and you are feeling hot, the chances are that you will be dehydrated. Drinks should be consumed before, during and after a training session/match, if possible. There are intervals during matches for players to take on fluid for rehydration – do not waste this opportunity. It is important not to become dehydrated, as this will affect health and performance. Netball players should ideally consume two litres of water before a match, two litres during a match and two litres after a match.

Check out some hydration facts by visiting http://news.bbc.co.uk/sport1/hi/health_and_fitness/4289412.stm

It is also important for players to avoid injury. You should always warm up by stretching your muscles and joints before beginning a game or a training session. This helps you to improve your flexibility and prevents you from straining muscles. The stretching exercises should be dynamic rather than static. It is also important to do some cool-down exercises after a game or training session. If you are just starting out in your netballing career, it is important to eat and train sensibly. The best thing to do is to join a local team or club, where you will receive coaching on playing skills, advice about the sort of exercise programme you should be following, and guidance on your diet.

What do I need to know if I want to start playing or watching netball?

You need to know the basics first: what the court is like, who the players are, the length of a match, who the match officials are and the scoring system. These are all explained in the rules of the game.

Remember that having the right attitude is just as important as having the correct equipment and knowing the rules.

Netball is about respecting the game and each other. Everyone involved with netball needs to remember how important the spirit of the game is. Treat other people in the way you would like to be treated and play to the best of your ability.

Here are some guidelines on acting within the spirit of the game:

- Recognise how well a member of your own side and the opposition is doing by applauding successes.
- Thank people involved with the match at the end of the game.
- Remember that there is no room for negative behaviour in netball. Do not try to distract opposing players by making unnecessary noise and do not criticise the way someone (either on your own team or the opposing team) is playing. Everyone is doing their best.
- Do not be rude or violent.
- Remember that players must respect the decisions of the umpires.

Netball should be about everyone enjoying themselves.

Summary

1 Netball can be enjoyed at many different levels by players of all ages and abilities. Netball is not just for girls; there is a growing number of male teams.

2 There are modified versions of netball for younger players, to help them develop those all-important ball skills and to promote having lots of fun.

3 You can join a school team or local side to receive coaching.

4 A healthy diet and sensible training programme are important if you want to develop your skills as a netball player. The best place to receive this advice is from a qualified coach.

5 The rules are all about playing fairly.

6 Netball is fun for everybody.

Training

A Keep a food diary for a week. Write down everything that you eat and drink. Make sure you are eating at least five portions of fruit and vegetables a day.

B Start to think about your level of fitness. It is important to build up your muscles and develop your fitness gradually, otherwise you risk injuring yourself. The best way to get fit is to join a local side. Here is a website that can help you to start finding out about what you need to do to get fit:

http://news.bbc.co.uk/ sport1/hi/health_and_ fitness/default.stm

C Look at the information provided in Chapter 10 to help you find a local side.

Chapter 4
The Basics

All about...a match

There are two teams of seven players. Each team tries to score as many goals as possible by passing the ball into the goal circle area of the court, where the goal shooter (GS) or goal attack (GA) can try to score a goal. A goal is scored by shooting the ball through the goal ring. The other side tries to prevent the opposition from passing the ball into the goal circle and from shooting successfully. It is a non-contact sport, so players rely on speed, agility and skill.

All about...the rules

- There are 21 netball rules, which have been developed since 1891, so that the game is fair and exciting to watch, as well as to play.
- The rules are the same whether players are amateur or professional. There are some modifications to the rules for players with a disability, and also some useful guidance for coaches and umpires working with deaf or hearing-impaired players.

 Find out more about rule modifications at www.england-netball.co.uk by selecting 'the game' menu button, followed by 'Disability'.

Rule 1 describes the court, the goalposts, the ball and the players.

Rule 2 explains the duration of the match, the way in which the time is divided into quarters and the intervals between each quarter. This rule also suggests how the length of the match can be amended, depending upon the age of the players and the number of matches that teams are expected to compete in during a day.

Rule 3 explains who the match officials are and what their roles are. It also explains the way in which the umpire should use the whistle to control the match and to communicate with players.

Rule 4 explains that a team is either male or female and that it must not be mixed (it is quite acceptable to train in mixed groups). It explains that there must be five team members present from each team for a game to take place. It identifies the different playing positions and describes how substitutes must be registered before the start of a match, but that there are no limits to the number of substitutions that can be made during a game.

Rule 5 describes the way in which players who have arrived late can take their place on the team through substitution, if someone has taken the player's place or provided that the team is a player down after a pause in the game, so long as the umpire has been informed. The rule also identifies the penalty for players coming onto the court before a pause in the match, or without informing the umpire.

Rule 6 explains what substitution and team change means. It describes how players can be substituted for one another and the penalties for not abiding by the rules for coming onto and off the court at the correct time.

Rule 7 describes stoppages in the event of injury or illness, as well as stoppages for obstruction, contact and the ball going out of the court. This rule also gives umpires the power to stop matches in an emergency.

Rule 8 describes the different playing areas that can be found on a netball court and identifies where the different playing positions are permitted to play.

Rule 9 describes what is meant by offside and what an umpire must do if a player is offside. It explains that it does not matter if the player has the ball or not. This rule is expanded upon in Rule 13 because players can reach into offside areas to retrieve the ball, provided their feet remain onside. This rule also explains that, if two players from opposing teams are offside, the umpire will allow play to continue if neither of the players has contact with the ball. Otherwise, a toss up will take place in the player's correct playing area.

Rule 10 explains what it means by the ball being 'out of court' and that there should be a throw-in to get the ball back into play. If the ball rebounds off the goalpost back into the court, it has not gone out of play. This rule also explains what the umpires should do if players go out of court for any reason other than to retrieve the ball for a throw-in.

Rule 11 explains the positions that players should be in before the start of play, and the penalties for players who are in the incorrect part of the court.

Rule 12 explains how a match should be started and restarted after every goal is scored with a centre pass.

Rule 13 explains when players can play the ball and the ways in which a ball should be controlled, as well as the fact that the ball must be played within three seconds of being caught, that there must be space for a third player between the player passing the ball and the player receiving the ball, and that the ball should not be thrown over a complete third without being touched by another player. It also describes the ways in which players must not handle the ball (eg hitting the ball with the fist) or use the goalpost to regain balance, or as a support.

Rule 14 is the footwork rule. It explains that, if a player catches the ball, the foot she lands on is called the landing foot and this foot must remain grounded during a pivot to change direction. The player is allowed to take a step but the ball must be released by the time the landing foot comes back to the ground, having been lifted to complete the stepping action.

Rule 15 is about scoring goals and how players who are eligible to score goals must have landed inside the goal circle, must not step outside the circle, must shoot within three seconds of receiving the ball, and must abide by the footwork rule.

Rule 16 explains what is meant by obstruction and intimidation, and outlines the penalties for these actions.

Rule 17 explains that netball is a non-contact sport and that players touching one another, accidentally or deliberately, will be penalised.

Rule 18 explains the different kinds of penalties that umpires can award and when they can be used.

Rule 19 explains that players should behave in a sporting and responsible manner. It identifies that players failing to live up to standards of fair play, such as deliberately wasting time or delaying the game, will be penalised.

Rule 20 explains how umpires can warn, suspend and order players off the court if they persistently break the rules or behave in an unsporting way.

Rule 21 explains what happens if a team fails to take to the court and outlines the penalties for not playing. If five players are available, then the game can go ahead but, if there are fewer than five players, the game is awarded to the team that is present.

A summary of the rules can be found on the England Netball website. If you want your own copy of the full rules, they can be purchased from Coachwise Ltd at www.1st4sport.com, quoting reference code BONR.

All about...the different organisations involved with netball

There are several organisations involved with netball. These organisations are called 'governing bodies'. They are responsible for regulating, promoting and organising tournaments, leagues and many age group competitions.

Table 1: The various netball organisations

Organisation	Role	Website
International Netball Federation (IFNA)	The governing body for world netball responsible for the rules of the game and promoting netball worldwide.	www.netball.org
Netball Europe (previously called The Federation of European Netball Associations – FENA)	There are seven affiliated members: England, Scotland, Northern Ireland, Wales, Republic of Ireland, Malta and Gibraltar. All these members are committed to developing netball and playing against each other. In 2006, Israel took part in the Netball Europe development competition.	www.netballeurope.org
England Netball	The governing body for netball in England, responsible for the development and support of netball from grass roots to elite levels.	www.england-netball.co.uk
Northern Ireland Netball	The governing body for netball in Northern Ireland.	www.houseofsportni.net
Netball Scotland	The governing body for netball in Scotland.	www.netballscotland.com
Welsh Netball Association	The governing body for netball in Wales.	www.welshnetball.co.uk

All about...the world rankings

IFNA World Rankings identify the teams that do best during a year.

Positions are allocated based on how well the different teams are doing.

Find out how well your favourite country is doing in the world rankings by visiting www.netball.org/IFNA.aspx?id=94

In the past, Australia and New Zealand's Silver Ferns have dominated the world rankings.

All about...netball in this country

Netball in this country is not a professional sport. Elite players or athletes, as they are called, can obtain funding, which allows them to work part-time so that they can be fully committed to developing their netball skills.

Elite athletes from England and Wales play in the Netball Super League (NSL). There are eight teams:

Brunel Hurricanes

Celtic Dragons

Leeds Met Carnegie

Loughborough Lightning

Mavericks

Northern Thunder

Team Bath

Team Northumbria

The Super League is also committed to developing netball at a regional level.

Find out more about some of the teams in the NSL here:

www.brunelhurricanes.co.uk
www.leedsmet.ac.uk
www.sportnorthumbria.com
www.teambath.com and
www.thundernetball.com

National Super League

Premier League. The league is made up of two divisions.

Regional Leagues. There are nine regions with their own leagues for open and junior age groups.

Winners from the regional leagues enter a play-off competition to gain a place in the second division of the Premier League, while the bottom team in the second division of the Premier League is relegated.

Regional clubs also have the opportunity to play in the Challenge Cup competition. This is a knockout competition rather like football's FA Cup, where clubs have an opportunity to play teams from neighbouring regions. As the tournament progresses, teams that have won earlier rounds have the chance to play teams from further afield. The more successful a team is, the more likely they are to draw a team from any of the nine regions.

Find out more about the netball leagues by visiting
www.england-netball.co.uk/events

What does 'open' mean?
An open competition is for players over 21.

Some important competitions
The World Netball Championships

All countries that have some form of membership within IFNA can take part in this tournament, which is held in July once every four years. The World Youth Championships are held in the same month but two years before the World Netball Championships. Early rounds are based on a pool system, played in a round-robin format. Teams play each other over a 12-day period, gaining points. There are two points available for a win and one point available for a draw. After the initial stages of the competition, the teams with the most points go forward to the quarter-finals. The four sides with the highest number of points progress to the semi-finals.

Commonwealth Games

This is an international tournament that IFNA wants to make as exciting as possible for the players and the spectators. Nations compete to score as many points as possible.

 Find out more about the Commonwealth Games at www.thecgf.com Click onto 'sports' and select 'netball' to find out who has achieved medal places in the Commonwealth Games.

Netball Europe Championships

This tournament is played by the members of Netball Europe.

Test Series

Top netballing nations compete against each other in a series of three matches. Test Series are often annual events.

All about...national netball centres

There are a number of national netball centres where the England squad trains and where the most promising players in the country can develop their skills. There are centres in Bath, Sheffield and Loughborough.

 Find out more about the national centres by visiting www.teambath.com/?page_ id=532 and http://sdc.lboro.ac.uk /facilities/netball/index.php? cat_id=18&subcat_id=46& level=2

Take a virtual tour of Sheffield's centre at: www.eis-sheffield.co.uk/content. php?nPageID=68

Summary

1 Netball is played at many different levels to suit all ages and abilities.

2 International events include the World Championships and the Commonwealth Games, where elite netball athletes compete against each other.

3 There is usually a Test Series played each year over three matches.

4 The governing bodies of netball are determined to improve the sport's profile. There are already a number of national netball centres where elite players can train and where developing players can improve their skills.

5 Teams play in leagues that vary according to the ability of the clubs and the players. This means that games are interesting to play and to watch.

Training

1 Find out about an NSL team near to where you live. Go to the England Netball site, select 'Events' and then 'Super League'.

2 Find out who is playing in your national squad.

3 Use the Internet to find out the following information:

a In which NSL teams do the current national squad players compete?

b Who is the current captain of the squad and where does she play?

c Who is the current national coach and assistant coach?

d Where are the next World Championships to be held? Look at the under-21 and the open-age group tournaments.

4 Find out about netball in some of the top ranking countries in the world.

Here's a link to get you started:

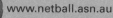 www.netball.asn.au

Chapter 5
The Ingredients of Netball

This chapter is about the essential components required for an official netball match.

All about...the court

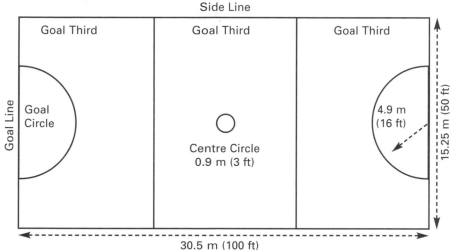

Figure 1: The netball court

The court is marked with white lines. These white lines show the boundaries of the court and the different areas on the court, as detailed below:

- The boundaries of the court are marked by **goal lines**, which are 15.25 m (50 ft) long and by **side lines** which are 30.5 m (100 ft) long.
- The court is divided by **transverse lines** marked across the court.
- The court is divided into thirds. There is one **centre third** and two **goal thirds** – one at each end of the court. Each team has a **defensive third**, where their defenders are placed to try and prevent their opponents from scoring goals, and an **attacking third**, where they hope to pass the ball, feeding it into the goal circle so that they can shoot and score a goal.

- The **goal circle** is actually a semi-circle. There is one at either end of the court. The goal circle has a radius of 4.9 m (16 ft). The goalpost is placed on the goal line midway between the end points of the goal circle. The goal circle is also called the **shooting circle**.
- The **centre circle** is in the middle of the court. It has a diameter of 0.9 m (3 ft). This is where the game is started and restarted from after a goal has been scored.
- The markings must not be more than 50 mm (2 ins) wide. This is important because the markings are part of the court and part of the different areas described. This means that, so long as a player still has her foot on the line, she is inside her area or inside the court.

The court must be made of a firm non-slip surface. There are different surfaces that can be used, especially if the surface will also be used for other things. Indoor courts sometimes have floors made from timber. Indoor courts must have clear space of at least 3.05 m (10 ft) all around the court. This is called the run-off. It is also important for indoor courts to have a minimum ceiling height of 8.3 m.

Netball Super League (NSL) must be played on a sprung floor, the posts must be padded and there must be run-offs provided beyond the lines of the court. The posts are also often sunk into the floor.

All about...the posts

- The goalposts must be vertical (upright).
- They must be 3.05 m (10 ft) tall.
- They must have a diameter measuring between 65 mm (2.5 ins) and 100 mm (49 ins).
- The goalposts are placed in the middle of each of the goal lines. The outer edge of the post is outside the goal line (ie off the court).
- The ring at the top of the post must be at the end of a firm post that is at right angles to the upright post, and which

projects 150 mm (6 ins) from the top of the post.
- The ring must have an internal diameter of 380 mm (15 ins). It must be fitted with a net that is open at both ends so that the ball can pass through it.
- A goal is scored (provided it is thrown by a player with that role in the correct position) if the ball passes 'over and completely through the ring'[1] and the net.

All about...the ball

The ball must:

- be spherical
- be made from leather, rubber or a synthetic material that has the same behaviour as the natural materials
- have a circumference of between 690 mm (27 ins) and 710 mm (28 ins)
- weigh between 400 g (14 oz) and 450 g (16 oz).

Netballs can be purchased in different sizes. A match ball is normally size 5.

What sort of ball should I choose for practice?

If you are a young player, you need to choose a ball that is right for your stage of growth. A size 4 ball is recommended for players between the ages of eight and 10. This will enable you to spread your fingers to cover the surface of the ball, so that you can practise the correct techniques for holding and passing the ball. The High 5 game of netball is played with a size 4 ball. Those aged 11 upwards can use a size 5 ball. Coaches may use pass-developer balls, which are heavier than standard balls and which have surfaces designed to be gripped. This type of ball is designed to improve passing skill and accuracy.

[1] Official Netball Rules, page 39

How do I know if the ball is correctly inflated?

When you are holding the ball, it should not feel soft or squashy – if there is too much give, it is not fully inflated and will not bounce properly.

All about...the players

- A match is played by two teams.
- There are 12 people in each team but only seven players from each team are allowed on the court at any one time.
- Each of the players on a team is given a position. All players wear bibs, which indicate their position. The bibs show the players' positions on the front and on the back. The bibs must be clearly visible. They must not be covered and they must not be below the waist. The letters must be at least 150 mm (6 ins) high.
- The positions are given by these abbreviated forms.

```
GK = Goal keeper
GD = Goal defence
WD = Wing defence
C  = Centre
WA = Wing attack
GA = Goal attack
GS = Goal shooter
```

- Players must be able to assume either attacking or defending tactics, but the playing position that a player is given will demand that he is better at some skills than others, depending upon the position. For example, a wing attack (WA) needs accurate ball-feeding skills among his repertoire of techniques.
- The player in the centre (C) position takes the centre pass to start a game or restart it after a goal has been scored. She is also the only player who is able to go into all three thirds of the court. The only place she is not allowed to go is in the two goal circles. This means that the centre (C) player has an important attacking and defending role. These players create opportunities and organise tactics.
- Players in different positions are only allowed into defined areas of the court. If they move into the wrong area of the court, they are offside and will be penalised. It does not matter if they have possession of the ball or not.

Substitutions

- The team is required to register five substitutes before the match. The team manager or head coach will do this when he submits the team sheet.
- There are no rules about the number of substitutions that can be made during a match.
- Substituted players can return to the game, provided that there are never more than seven players on the court from one team at any one time.
- Substitutions are made during intervals or stoppages (only if there is an injured player who needs replacing, or if the opponents have called a 'time out', meaning the opposing coach can then substitute or change any of the players). It is not necessary to tell the other team that these substitutions have been made, however, it is important to follow the

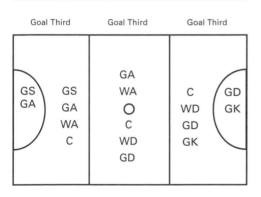

Goal Third   Goal Third   Goal Third

proper procedures for entering or leaving the game. There are penalties for coming onto the court or leaving it incorrectly. More about this in Chapter 6 and Chapter 9.

All about...what players wear

- Female players usually wear a T-shirt and skirt, or a dress. Male players wear a T-shirt and shorts.
- All players wear a coloured bib that identifies their playing position on both the front and the back.
- Players should not wear jewellery unless it takes the form of a wedding ring or a medical alert bracelet. In either case, they should be taped so that they do not cause injury to anyone else. It is for this reason that netball players are required to keep their nails short and smooth.

© Action Images

Choosing a pair of trainers

Remember that you will need footwear that has a good grip on a hard surface. Players must not wear spikes as this would be unfair, as well as dangerous, for other players. If you are playing on an indoor surface, it is important to have good grip, but to not mark the surface of the court. It is also important to choose trainers that have plenty of cushioning to protect you as you run and jump on the court, as well as support to enable quick turning. Netball players need to be agile and run quickly, so it is also important that the trainers you choose should be lightweight.

As you become more interested in netball, your coach will advise you about suitable footwear. England Netball recommends that players buy Asics netball training shoes – see Chapter 3 for more guidance about footwear.

All about...where the players are allowed to go on the court

Players are permitted to go only into the thirds and goal circles designated by their playing positions.

All about...the defenders

- **Goal keepers** (GK) must try to prevent the ball from being successfully passed by their opponents and must also attempt to defend against goal shots. The goalkeeper is only permitted to stay inside his own goal third (the defensive third), including the goal circle.
- **Goal defence** (GD) players mark the opposing team's goal attack (GA) during man-to-man marking. They also defend the goal. It is the job of a player in goal defence to stop the goal attack from

scoring a goal, and also to gain the ball. Players in a goal defence position are able to play in the defensive third, including the goal circle. They are also allowed to play in the centre third. As well as defending and denying space, the goal defence must try to pass the ball to attacking players on his own team.

- **Wing defence** (WD) players try to prevent the opposing wing attack (WA) from receiving the ball and passing it to the goal shooter (GS) or the goal attack. This player also has an attacking role because, once the wing defence has possession of the ball, she must try to pass the ball to create opportunities for her team to attack and score a goal. Wing defenders are allowed in the centre third and their defensive third, but they are not permitted into the goal circle.

All about...the attackers

- **Wing attack** (WA) players try to pass the ball or feed the ball into the goal circle to give the goal shooter or the goal attack an opportunity to score a goal. The wing attack is the main player responsible for receiving the centre pass and feeding the ball to the shooters. Wing attacks are allowed in the centre third and their opponent's goal third, but they are not allowed in the goal circle. Wing attackers need to develop accurate feeding skills so that they can pass the ball to their goal shooter and goal attack.

- **Goal shooter** (GS) players must shoot to score goals or pass the ball to the goal attack, if this player is in a better position to score. Goal shooters are only permitted to play in their opponent's goal third. They are also allowed inside the goal circle so they can try to score goals.

- **Goal attack** (GA) players work with the attacking players to ensure that the ball is passed into the goal circle. They are also allowed to try to score goals. The goal attack is able to play in the centre third and her opponent's goal circle.

Top tip: Only players allowed inside their opponent's goal circle are allowed to score goals. All those players with a 'G' on their bib will be allowed into one of the goal circles.

All about...the umpires

Each netball match is overseen by two umpires. The umpires make sure that the match is played fairly. It is a very serious offence for a player to disagree or argue with an umpire.

The umpires:

- make sure that the court is in a suitable condition for the match to be played and that the goalposts have been set up properly
- are responsible for ensuring that the match ball meets the specifications set down in the rules and that the players are correctly attired
- make sure that the correct time is taken for intervals and each quarter of play
- start and stop the game by blowing a whistle
- administer the rules and give penalties or free passes where the rules are broken
- make decisions on events that are not covered by the rules. This means that they ensure that matches are played fairly in the true spirit of the game
- use a number of specified hand signals to communicate decisions.

In official matches, there will also be scorers and timekeepers off the court. It is the two umpires' job to communicate goals and stoppages, as well as restarts, to the correct person. This is done by using a whistle.

Each umpire is responsible for one half of the court and one whole length of a side line.

Umpire profile
Bill Alexander is one of England's top umpires and so knows all about the netball rules. Bill has a reputation for being tough on offenders. As well as umpiring Super League matches in England, Bill also umpires at international tournaments such as the 2006 Commonwealth Games.

Find out more about what it takes to be a netball umpire at www.netballonline.com/umpiring.php

To find out about the current list of international umpires, visit IFNA's website at www.netball.org/Netball.aspx?id=19

All about...the timekeepers and scorers

In official matches, timekeepers:

- tell the umpire when there are 30 seconds until the start of the game
- use a stopwatch to keep time when the umpire blows her whistle to start the match
- hold and restart time if the umpire stops the match. This will be signalled by the umpire blowing her whistle
- keep and record time for any stoppage time or injury time
- ensure that stoppage time is played in the quarter or half in which the stoppage occurred
- signal the end of the quarter to the umpire so that she can call time
- keep time for intervals.

In official matches, scorers:

- record centre passes
- record goals as they are scored
- record any suspensions or the names of any players ordered off the court
- record substitutions (in Super League games and Test matches)
- tell the umpire who had the last centre pass if she needs to check
- check the scores.

All about...the length of a match

- A match lasts for 60 minutes (an hour).
- It is divided into four quarters of 15 minutes each. The teams change ends after each quarter.
- The half-time interval is five minutes. There are intervals of three minutes between the other quarters. Players go to a designated team bench area at these times.
- The rules permit the length of the match to be amended, depending on the age of the players and the number of matches to be played in one day. If teams are playing in several matches over one day, the match can be reduced to 40 minutes. This means that each quarter is 10 minutes long.

All about...winning

© Mark Pritchard

- The side with the most goals wins. Goals can only be scored by the goal shooter and the goal attack. They must be inside the goal circle before shooting at the goal. The ball must pass through the metal hoop and the net for a goal to be scored.

Summary

1 There are two teams. Each team has seven players on the court. Each of the players wears a bib showing their playing positions.

2 The five substitutes must be identified before the match – this means that there are 12 people on the team.

3 The substitutes can be substituted for players who are on the court during intervals and stoppages.

4 Players who have left the court become substitutes and can be returned to the game. There are no limits to the number of substitutions that can be made. This means that substitution is a tactic used by coaches to ensure that the best players are in position throughout the match.

5 It is important for players to ensure that they are wearing trainers that support and cushion their feet.

6 The team that gains possession of the ball tries to pass the ball into the goal circle, so that the goal shooter or the goal attack can shoot at the goal. If the ball passes through the goal ring, a goal is scored, provided the shot was made by the goal shooter or the goal attack.

7 Players are allowed in defined areas of the court. If they move out of the area of the court they should be in, they are offside. More about this in Chapter 8.

8 There are two umpires who have control of the game. Each umpire controls half the court and one of the side lines. It is not acceptable to disagree with the umpires.

9 Matches are an hour long. The time is split into quarters with a five-minute interval at half-time and a three-minute interval between the other quarters.

10 The team that scores the most goals wins.

Training

A Here is a partially completed plan of a netball court.

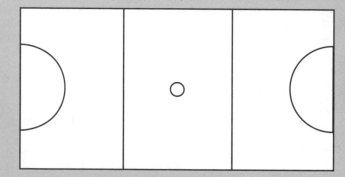

   i Label the different areas on the court.

  ii Identify the area that each umpire is responsible for.

B i Workout what the player abbreviations stand for.

  ii Identify the thirds that these players are allowed to use.

Player	Full name of position	Defensive third	Centre third	Attacking third
GS				
GA				
WA				
C				
WD				
GD				
GK				

  iii Identify which players are allowed in the goal circle that they are defending.

  iv Identify which players are allowed in the goal circle that they are attacking.

C Watch a netball match.

   i Identify the different features on the court.

  ii Note down the different umpire signals you see being used.

  iii Look at the way in which players are substituted. When do substitutions occur? Why do you think they are made?

Chapter 6

Following the Progress of a Match

Before the match, a coin is tossed. The winner either decides which end of the court they wish to attack or whether to take the first centre pass.

↓

The two centre (C) players are the only players allowed in the centre third before play begins. All the other players should be in their own thirds. It does not matter where they are, as long as they are on the correct side of the transverse lines. The centre taking the centre pass must be in the centre circle. The other centre must be outside the circle and must not be obstructing the player with the ball. All the other players must be in their own goal thirds.

↓

The umpire blows her whistle to start the match.

↓

The centre with the ball must pass it within three seconds of the whistle being blown. She must also remember to obey the footwork rule, which is described in the technical rules section of this chapter. If these rules are infringed, a free pass is awarded. The players who are allowed to play in the centre third come into the area to catch or intercept the ball. The players allowed inside the centre third are the GA, WA, C, WD and GD players. The ball must be caught within the centre third.

↓

The player who catches the ball must remember the footwork rule and only take one step, having caught the ball. The ball must be released within three seconds of being caught.

The ball cannot be passed straight into the attacking third of the court. It must be passed to another player or be touched by another player in the same third before it can be passed across the transverse line. This means that, if the ball is in the defensive third, it cannot be passed straight into the attacking third.

↓

A pattern of passes develops until the ball is fed into the goal or shooting circle. The goal shooter (GS) and goal attack (GA) are the only players who can shoot and score goals. The player scoring must be inside this semi-circle.

↓

Defenders must not make contact with attackers and they must remain 90 cm (3 ft) away from the player with the ball. This means that defenders can only try to gain possession when the ball is in the air during an attempted pass. The ball can be thrown in any manner and in any direction.

↓

A goal is scored when the ball is passed down through the ring and net. If the ball rebounds from the goalpost, the goal shooter or the goal attack can shoot again, if they are able to do so, because Rule 10 explains that 'a ball which hits any part of the goalpost and rebounds into play, is not out of court'.[2]

↓

Play is restarted with a centre pass from the centre circle. The throw is taken first by one side and then by the other. It alternates.

[2] Official Netball Rules, page 28

21

The umpire blows her whistle at the end of the quarter and raises her arm straight above her head to call time (or the end of the match).

When the match restarts, the teams will change ends. The centre pass alternates between the two teams. If a team scores just before the final whistle of a period, but does not have the opportunity to take their centre pass, it will be this team that takes the centre pass.

The umpire signalling 'time'.

 If a player catches a centre pass, can they be on the transverse line? The player must land with their landing foot inside the centre third. The rules are very clear about this. It is not acceptable to land on both feet with one on either side of the transverse line, and it is not acceptable for the landing foot to be inside the goal third and for the trailing foot to land in the centre third. The importance of the landing point is for receivers who are on the thrower's team.

If a defender touches the ball first, the umpire will not look to see which foot the player landed on first.

Are players allowed to run with the ball? No. The ball must be passed. The rules are very clear about ball control. Read on to find out more about ball control.

Player profile
Chioma Ezeogu, of the Brunel Hurricanes and England, has represented her country since 1998 and so has a developed arsenal of dodges and fast-sprint tactics.

© SW Pix

Playing the game

The netball rules are designed to ensure a fast-paced and action-filled game. They are also designed to ensure fair play, Infringements either result in a free pass or a penalty pass. If an umpire awards a penalty pass against a player, it means that the player can take no part in the game while the penalty pass is being taken. Rules resulting in a penalty pass or shot at goal if they are infringed are simple – do not touch other players even by accident and do not try to move the netball post to make scoring goals easier! Players must also remember not to obstruct their opponents. If an opposing player has the ball, it is important to be more than 0.9 m (3 ft) away from her or else you are obstructing, and a penalty pass will be awarded against your team.

The rules resulting in a free pass, if they are infringed, are sometimes called technical rules because they are about the way in which the game must be played. There are very few of them compared to some other sports, but they are all very important and netball players need to know them and abide by them throughout the game.

Infringement of rules, resulting in a free pass

They are important rules because they are about ball control, the length of time that the ball can be held for, footwork and making space.

The three-second rule

- Players can only hold the ball for three seconds before they have to pass the ball. This makes the game exciting to watch and to play.

Ball control

Rule 13 describes the ways in which players can and cannot play the ball.

Here are some of the things that players have to remember:

- Balls may be caught or thrown with one or two hands.
- Players must be on their feet when they throw or catch the ball. This means that, if you fall, you must be back on your feet before passing the ball.
- Players can bounce or 'bat' the ball once to gain control of it before they pass it. However, the bounce must not begin by the ball being thrown into the air. As soon as the ball is pushed or thrown into the air, it is considered to be passed. If the player who pushed the ball into the air then bounces it, she will have fallen foul of the rule regarding space and will be penalised.
- If the ball is on the ground, players can roll the ball along the ground so that they can then gain possession.
- Once a player has had contact with the ball, she is allowed no further contact

until another player has caught or touched the ball.
- Players are not allowed to run with or dribble the ball.

 Catching and keeping hold of the ball is a basic skill that every netball player needs to master. Watch the ball; reach out towards it – your arms should be extended to their full length. Be prepared to stretch or jump so that you get to the ball first. Spread your fingers so that you are covering a larger surface area of the ball and make sure that your thumbs are touching so that the ball will not continue on its journey through your hands. Think of your hands as being like a giant cup to catch the ball: in netball, the hand shape is called 'making a w'.

Figure 2: Making a 'W'

Once you have caught the ball, bring it in towards your chest to prevent it from falling and also to cushion it ready for the throw.

Remember that you must release the ball within three seconds of catching it.

Top tip: Anticipate where the ball is going to be so that you can jump or stretch towards it to gain possession.

What happens if a player catches and then drops the ball?

The ball must be caught or touched by another player. The player cannot catch the ball again or tip it to another player. If she does this, it would be replaying the ball, which is illegal and would result in a free pass to the opposing team.

Passing distance

• When the ball is passed, there must be enough space for another player to move between the thrower and the catcher. This is designed to prevent very close passes, which would be unfair and also not very interesting for spectators to watch.

Footwork

The footwork rule is unique to netball. Put quite simply, it means that netball players catch the ball and are allowed to take only one step before passing the ball. It is important to master this rule if you want to be a successful netball player.

• When a player lands after catching the ball, the foot that they land on is called the 'landing foot'.
• The player can choose to keep this foot grounded and can pivot on it to change direction.
• Alternatively, a player can make a step with his other foot, lift the landing foot and throw the ball before the landing foot returns to ground. In actual fact, this means that players make one step and three-quarters before releasing the ball.
• If a player moves his landing foot in any other way during this stage of the pass, then he has broken the rule. This is called stepping and will result in a free pass. More about this in Chapter 9.

What happens if a player lands on both feet?

The player can decide which is the landing foot but must then follow the rules above.

Pivoting is an important part of a netball player's skill. The pivot allows players to change direction quickly so that they can pass the ball into a clear space. Remember that you must keep your landing foot grounded.

• Bend your knees and keep your weight low to help maintain balance. Stay on the balls of your feet.
• Pivot on the ball of your foot by pushing off with the other foot. This simply means that you step to the right using the left leg across your body (assuming that your landing foot is the right foot).
• You can keep stopping and pushing off with your left foot as long as you keep the landing foot (the right one) firmly grounded. The only other thing to remember is the direction you are travelling in. If you have landed on your right foot then pivot clockwise – to the right. If you've landed on your left foot, pivot anti-clockwise. Remember that the best place to learn and develop these skills is at a club, where you will receive advice and coaching.

A netball player illustrating the pivoting action.

If you watch elite players, you will see that they do not simply remain stationary, pivot or step. They take the simple movements required by the footwork rule and turn them into something much more athletic.

Learn more about landing and footwork by visiting http://news.bbc.co.uk/sport1/hi/other_sports/netball/4187508.stm

More about playing the ball

There are several different types of pass that netball players use. The reason for this is that the ball is moved by passing. Different kinds of passes will have different effects on the ball. For example, an overhead pass should pass through the air above the defenders' outstretched hands, whereas an underarm pass should be a short and accurate pass.

Types of pass

Two-handed pass	One-handed pass
Chest pass	Shoulder pass
Overhead pass	Underarm pass
Lob	

 Bounce passes can be one- or two-handed.

Two-handed passes are the easiest to control, so this is a good place to begin. The chest pass allows players to draw the caught ball towards them to cushion it and then to propel it forwards. Remember that the time between catching the ball and passing it should be no more than three seconds.

- Stand so that you are well-balanced. Your feet should be in line with your shoulders. Draw the ball in towards you so that your elbows are in and your hands are behind the ball. The ball should be at chest height.
- Make sure that your fingers are spread into a 'w' shape behind the ball.
- Keep your eye on your target.
- Propel the ball away from you by transferring your weight forwards. Push your arms forwards and use your wrists to add to the lift.

- The ball should be given direction by the turn of your fingers.

© Action Images

Demonstration of a chest pass.

 Find out more about the skills you need to play netball at: www.netballfun.com/tips.html

If you want to be a successful netball player, then you will need to develop your throwing skills so that you can throw accurately over different distances, depending on the situation you find yourself in. The best way to develop these skills is by joining a club, where you will receive advice and coaching, as well as plenty of practice as part of a team.

© Action Images/Reuters

Player profile

Jade Clarke plays in a wing defence or centre position, and so understands that throwing skills are essential and that players need a range of them, depending on the situation in which they find themselves. She has honed her throwing skills during Test Series with New Zealand, Jamaica and, in 2005, South Africa. She was also a member of the Melbourne Commonwealth Games 2006 squad.

Out of court

It is inevitable that sometimes players will misjudge throwing distance or will fail to catch the ball. If it lands inside the court, a player will gain possession and play continues. However, as soon as the ball touches the ground or anything outside the court, including players who are out of the court (outside the side lines and the goal lines), it is out of play.

Top tip: It is perfectly acceptable for a player inside the court to stop the ball from landing out of the court by leaning over the line and catching it. It is also acceptable to lean over the line and bat the ball back onto the court. The most important thing to remember is that the ball must not have touched anyone or anything outside the court.

What happens if the ball rebounds off the goalpost?

Play continues, so long as the ball rebounds into the court. If it rebounds out of the court, it can still be played, as long as a player leans across the goal or side line and returns it to play before it touches the ground.

More about scoring goals

The only attacking players allowed inside the goal circle are the goal shooter (GS) and goal attack (GA) players. It is important for these players to have quick reflexes, to be able to play creatively and also to be able to cope with the pressure of the position.

Players who are able to score goals need to remember these rules:

- All the other rules such as footwork and obstruction still apply inside the goal circle.
- In order to shoot at the goal, players must be completely inside the goal circle.
- If the ball bounces or rebounds from the goalpost, attacking players may try to retrieve the ball and score.

- If another player, other than the goal attack or goal shooter, puts the ball through the ring for whatever reason, no goal is scored and play is allowed to continue, so the attacking players need to retrieve the ball as quickly as possible and take a shot at the goal.

Only the goal shooter and the goal attack can score goals. They must be inside the goal circle and they must be able to avoid the defenders. Margaret Caldow of Australia and Jean Pierre of Trinidad and Tobago developed different techniques for shooting the ball, so that it is released high and accurately.

Stand with both feet on the ground – shoulder-width apart – so that you are well-balanced. You should be facing the goalpost and you should be focused on the rim of the net. The ball should be held with the fingers rather than the palm, and they should be underneath the ball to propel it upwards. Bend the knees, draw the arm back slightly so that the energy will travel up through the body, and then push the ball upwards, aiming to place it over the rim of the post. Think of a spring as your legs straighten and your arm follows through, followed by your wrist and fingers, which should be guiding the ball. Look at these diagrams to get a better idea of the importance of taking aim, of gathering energy and then releasing it in a controlled and accurate way. The best place to develop your shooting skills is at a club, where you will receive coaching and advice.

Figure 3: The high release shot

Player profile

An Australian legend, **Margaret Caldow**, made her first appearance on the world stage in 1963, before going on to captain the Australian team. She played in three winning World Championship teams and her method of shooting is now a standard technique. She has coached Australia and England.

Find out how to shoot accurately at http://news.bbc.co.uk/sport1/hi/other_sports/netball/4187548.stm

Summary

1 Matches are started and restarted by a centre pass. The two centres alternate who takes the pass.

2 Players must work as a team to pass the ball to their goal circle, where the goal attack and goal shooter are the only two players who can shoot and score goals.

3 All players must make sure that they know and abide by the rules, which result in a free pass, if they are infringed. These rules include the three-second rule, which dictates that players must pass the ball within three seconds of catching it, and the footwork rule, which means that they can take the maximum of one step before passing the ball.

4 Netball is a game of skill, speed and agility. These skills are best mastered at a club, where you will receive coaching and advice.

Training

A i What is this player doing?

ii Which part of the court is the player in?

iii Which of these players is not allowed inside the goal circle?

Wing attack ☐

Goal attack ☐

Goal shooter ☐

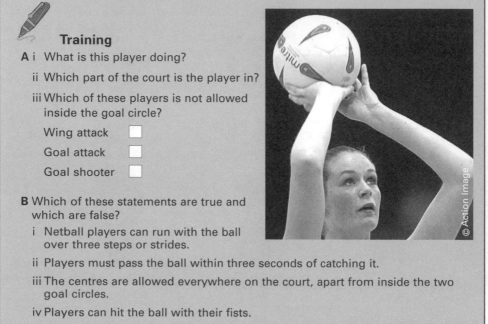

B Which of these statements are true and which are false?

i Netball players can run with the ball over three steps or strides.

ii Players must pass the ball within three seconds of catching it.

iii The centres are allowed everywhere on the court, apart from inside the two goal circles.

iv Players can hit the ball with their fists.

v Players must make sure that they are not standing within 0.9 m (3 ft) of their opponents if they are in possession of the ball.

Chapter 7
Attacking and Defending Play

Netball is about throwing and catching the ball, moving the ball through the court as a result of good linkage between players, keeping possession of the ball and scoring goals. Attackers try to feed the ball into the goal circle, so that the goal shooter (GS) or goal attack (GA) can shoot at the goal and score. Defenders try to stop this by intercepting passes and by preventing attacking players from being in a position that is clear of a defender. Each player has a restricted playing area. Only the centre (C) players have access to the whole court, with the exception of the goal circles. In order to play successfully, individual players must work as a team to pass the ball down the court and then feed it into the goal circle, or to block passes and retrieve the ball from the opposition.

Attacking play

The attacking team is the one in possession of the ball. Attacking players need to be available to receive passes – this is called 'getting free.' This means that they need to get away from defenders who are marking them and denying them the space to receive passes. They need to be able to 'get free' into a space, anticipating a teammate's need to pass the ball.

Methods of getting free

The aim is to get free of the opponent who is marking you.

This can be done by:

- sprinting into a clear, unmarked space on the court
- dodging a marker by moving one way and then quickly going in another direction
- a change in pace
- pivoting and changing direction

- suddenly stopping; you can then change direction or, as your marker slows down, sprint off in the same direction as before
- holding a space.

Top tip: Attackers need to take positive action. It is important to keep moving to stay free of your marker and to hold space, if necessary, until a teammate is able to pass the ball in your direction.

Methods of holding space

Holding or protecting a space means that the attacker is stopping the defender from taking a space that will enable her to catch the ball.

This can be done by:

- being in front of the marker
- facing the defender and then turning suddenly to catch the ball
- taking a step into the protected space to catch the ball as it is thrown.

Top tip: Communication is essential. Teams need to be able to communicate by looks and gestures, rather than by words.

Player profile

A Wigan-born PE teacher, **Karen Atkinson**, knows how to dominate the centre third. Accustomed to playing wing attack, wing defence or centre, she has been capped more than 50 times since captaining the England under-18s in 1995. She, along with her England teammates, gained a bronze medal in 1998 when she played in the World Netball Championships in New Zealand. Since then, Karen has represented her country at many a showpiece occasion, such as the Melbourne Commonwealth Games, where she again won a bronze medal.

Click on the 'finding space' video link at http://news.bbc.co.uk/sport1/hi/other_sports/netball/default.stm if you wish to learn more about netball masterclasses.

Defending play

Defenders must stop players in possession of the ball, so that they are unable to progress into the goal third and, from there, to the goal circle. This is achieved by marking the players from the other team.

- Defenders must prevent attacking players from gaining space that will be useful for receiving a pass.
- They must delay players from moving forward after they have thrown the ball.
- They also want to gain possession of the ball so that they, in turn, can become attackers. This is called intercepting the ball.

Remember that it is acceptable to be closer than 0.9 m (3 ft) to an opponent, so long as you are not involved in active play. Of course, the aim of the defender is to prevent the attacker from joining in with active play.

Man-to-man marking

Close marking means that an attacking player is not in a good position to receive the ball, because there is every chance that the ball will fall into the hands of the defending player.

A defender is best-placed in front of the attacking player so that her right shoulder is immediately in front of the left shoulder of her opponent. The defender's body angle must also be open to see the ball and the player being marked. The defender should be well-balanced and have her knees slightly bent in readiness for fast movement to intercept the ball or in readiness for an attempt by the attacker to create space.

Top tip: Defenders need to be alert and they need to move quickly.

Defending a player with the ball

Defending players in this situation can use their arms to try and cover the possible path of the ball, or they can jump and try to recover the ball as a result of anticipating the release and flight of the ball.

Defenders must remember the following, when the attacking player has the ball:

- If the opponent has the ball, the defender must be careful to be at least 0.9 m (3 ft) away from the leading foot of the player with the ball. Do not infringe this rule or else the defending player will be awarded a penalty pass or shot.
- Do not touch the ball while it is still in the hands of the other player. This is contact and a penalty pass or shot will be awarded against you.
- If a penalty pass or shot is awarded against a defender, the penalised player cannot take part in active play while the pass or shot is being made, which means that the penalised player cannot even call out or communicate in any way with her teammates.

Defending inside the goal circle

The goalkeeper and goal defence are the only defending players allowed inside the goal circles. The goal defence will mark the goal attack. Outside the goal circle, the goal defence will try to prevent the goal attack from moving into space that will lead her into the goal circle, while the goalkeeper will try to prevent the goal shooter from receiving the ball at all. However, if the goal shooter or the goal attack do gain possession of the ball in the goal circle, the two defending players must defend a shot at goal.

Defending the goal

The attacking player has a clearly defined target. The defender needs to be in front of the target, making sure that he is 0.9 m (3 ft) away from the leading foot of the attacking player. Lean upwards and forwards to cover the expected flight path of the ball. It is recommended to adopt a two-footed stance with flexed knees on the balls of your feet, to allow for sufficient elevation if a defender chooses to jump to intercept the shot. More advanced players sometimes prefer to take their weight on their front foot and lean upwards and forwards, using the other foot to keep balance and help with the gain in height. Players need to be able to hold these defending positions for three seconds, until the ball is released. Remember that the best place to learn these skills is at a club, where you will receive coaching and advice.

Player profile

Rachel Dunn is a part-time coach who has a vast understanding of the game. She held the key position of goal shooter at the 2006 Melbourne Commonwealth Games and received a bronze medal for her teamwork and accurate shooting skills. She has developed her skills against some of the best netball athletes in the world, having toured Australia and New Zealand, as well as playing in Test matches against these great netballing nations.

© Mark Pritchard

Find out more about attacking and defending by visiting http://news.bbc.co.uk/sport1/ hi/other_sports/netball/ default.stm

 What happens when two players from opposing teams get the ball at the same time or the umpire cannot see who reached the ball first?

It is almost inevitable that sometimes two players will reach the ball at the same time.

A toss-up is used to decide possession of the ball where players from opposing teams have simultaneously gained possession of the ball. For more information about the toss-up, read the section in Chapter 9 on page 42.

Summary

1 The seven players on each team have designated playing areas. This means that, no matter how talented one player is, the individuals must play as a team in order to be successful.

2 Attacking players must try to create space to receive the ball. They must use their judgement as to where the ball should be passed next. They must make progress down the court so that the ball can be fed into the goal circle for a shot at goal.

3 Defending players mark their opponents, in order to prevent them from receiving the ball, to intercept the ball and to prevent the attacking team from gaining ground.

4 Man-to-man marking means that the defender should effectively be restricting the attacking player's movements and denying her possession of the ball.

5 Players defending the player with the ball must be 0.9 m (3 ft) from the landing foot of the attacking player. Defenders will try to gain height in order to block the possible flight path of the ball.

6 Defending players must not touch the ball while it is still in the hands of the other player.

7 The best place to learn throwing, catching, attacking and defensive skills is at a club, where you will receive advice, coaching and plenty of practice as part of a team.

Training

A Look at these pictures of two players. In both cases, decide whether the umpire should penalise the defending player.

© Mark Pritchard

© Mark Pritchard

B Explain your answers to part A. What reasoning were your umpiring decisions based on?

C Watch a netball match.

  i Take note of the way in which defenders mark attacking players.

  ii Look at the different techniques that attacking players use to get free and move into space, so that they can gain possession of the ball.

Chapter 8

Offside, Obstructions and Other Infringements

Offside

All players need to remember which thirds of the court they are allowed to play in. These areas are known as the designated playing areas. Umpires watch to make sure players remain in their designated zones and quickly signal if a player crosses a transverse line into the wrong third, or goes into the goal circle when they are not permitted to be there.

The umpire signalling for offside.

There are three parts to the offside rule:

Part 1: A single player is offside. It does not matter if a player has the ball or not. If a player is in the wrong third of the court or has entered the goal circle when she should not have done, she is offside, and will be penalised. This rule even applies if players are taking throw-ins to return the ball into the game. A player must be outside the court and in line with her designated playing area, or she will be penalised. The umpire will award a free pass.

Part 2: If players from opposing teams are offside, it is called a 'simultaneous offside' and the rules are slightly different:

• **neither player touches the ball** – the umpire will allow play to continue
• **one of the offside players has the ball** – the umpire will return the players to the third in which they should be playing, and a toss-up is conducted between the two players

• **both the players have the ball** – the umpire will return them to the third in which they should be playing, and a toss-up is conducted between the two players. There is more about the toss-up in Chapter 9.

 What happens if two opposing players are simultaneously offside but neither of the players is allowed in the same third as the other?

The umpire will conduct a toss-up in the centre third between two players from opposing teams who are allowed to be in that third.

 Why is the offside rule different depending on whether there is one player or two players from opposing sides involved in a simultaneous offside?

The rules are all about playing fairly. If one player strays offside, then the opposition is at a disadvantage. If both teams have a player offside, it depends on whether they are interfering with the game or not. If they are not, the umpire plays the advantage. If either of the offside players have the ball, then the players need to be returned to their designated playing areas as fairly and as quickly as possible.

Part 3: It is perfectly acceptable for a player to retrieve the ball from a third that is outside her designated playing area, as long as her feet remain inside the correct zone.

Obstructions

Defending players must be at least 0.9 m (3 ft) away from the attacking player with the ball if they are going to try to intercept the ball, defend as the ball is thrown to another player or defend a shot at goal. If the rule is infringed, the umpire will award a penalty pass to the other team.

The umpire will signal that there has been an obstruction before penalising the player involved.

The three signals for obstruction.

How to measure the distance between players:

- It is important for defending players to be aware of where the attacking player's landing foot is positioned. This spot is the place they need to be 0.9 m (3 ft) from.
- If a defending player jumps to intercept the ball but lands closer than 0.9 m (3 ft), she is creating an obstruction.

 Are there any occasions when a defending player can be closer than 0.9 m (3 ft) to the attacking player with the ball?

Yes. Rule 16.3 is very clear:

'A player may be within 0.9 m of an opponent in possession of the ball, providing no effort is made to intercept or defend the ball, and there is no interference with that opponent's throwing or shooting action.'[3]

If a defender does interfere with play, she will not be on the court for very long! It is important for players to concentrate on the game and always be looking to gain possession of the ball.

Does the 0.9 m (3 ft) rule apply to players who do not have the ball? No. Players need to remember that this rule only applies if an opponent has the ball.

© Mark Pritchard

Player profile

Geva Mentor knows all about the importance of strong defensive play. As a goalkeeper/goal defence, she has gradually come up through the system and, in 2000, was rewarded for her hard work with a place in the national squad. In 2002, she was part of the team that won the European Championships. The Team Bath player has been part of the national squad ever since, and has played in the 2002 Manchester Commonwealth Games, the 2003 World Netball Championships in Jamaica, and the 2006 Melbourne Commonwealth Games where, like the rest of the squad, she won a bronze medal.

[3] Official Netball Rules, page 43

Other infringements

The tactics used by players depend on the kind of match they are playing. Netball is a fast, action-packed game. It is important to remember not to intimidate players from the opposing team, nor to make any contact with them. It is also important to remember the technical rules that were described in Chapter 6.

The technical rules: a reminder

Players must not hold the ball for longer than three seconds and they must make sure that their footwork complies with the rules, otherwise the umpire will award a free pass to the other team.

Netball is a **non-contact** sport. Players must not touch their opponents on purpose or accidentally. The rules are clear about the need for umpires to make judgements, based on principles of fair play. This means that players must not move into a position that will mean that the player who has just jumped to catch the ball will land on them. There must be no pushing, holding or leaning on an opponent either! The umpire will signal if contact has been made, by indicating where the contact occurred (in the diagram below, the umpire is signalling that contact has been made on the shoulder).

Umpire signalling 'footwork'.

Intimidation of any kind is not allowed. The umpire will award a penalty pass or penalty shot against the offender.

Summary

1 Players must remain in the areas designated by their playing positions. If they leave these areas, they are offside.

2 It does not matter whether the player who is offside is in possession of the ball or not.

3 If two players from opposing teams are simultaneously offside, the umpire will return the players to the third they should be in and conduct a toss-up to decide who has possession of the ball.

4 If the two opposing players cannot take the toss-up because neither of them is permitted into the other's third, then the toss-up is taken from the centre third by two players who are permitted in that zone.

5 Players must be 0.9 m (3 ft) away from their opponents. Players who are closer are obstructing the other players, unless they are taking no part in the game.

6 The distance between players is measured along the ground. If one of the players has possession of the ball, the distance is measured from the spot where her foot landed.

7 It is against the rules to intimidate another player.

8 Players must not have any contact with one another – either accidentally or deliberately. The umpire will make his decision based on the actions of the player who has been touched. If the player has come too close to the player who has made contact, or has filled the space that the player was clearly going for, then the obstruction rule is used.

9 It is important for players to remember the three-second rule and the footwork rule. If these rules are infringed, a free pass can be awarded against the offending players.

Training

A Look at these umpire signals.

i Identify the offence.

	Umpire's signal	Meaning
a		
b		
c		
d		
e		

ii Which two of the offences in the table above would result in a penalty pass or shot at goal?

B Watch a netball match. Do you agree with the umpire's decisions?

Chapter 9
Playing Advantage, Penalties and Other Sanctions

Netball is a fast-moving game based on fair play. Players value one another and the spectators. They also respect the umpires and the decisions that the umpires make during a match. The rules of netball are clear about what is fair and unfair.

If an umpire sees an infringement of the rules, she will stop play and state the action to be taken, such as a free pass, penalty pass or a toss-up. Players must make sure that they follow the umpire's instructions carefully. The umpire will indicate where the penalty is to be taken from. The different penalties are a free pass, penalty pass, penalty pass or shot, throw-in or toss-up. The umpire also has the opportunity to play an advantage if the team that has been infringed against has possession of the ball.

Get some tips about tactics, by visiting http://newsvote.bbc.co.uk/ sportacademy/hi/sa/netball/ features/newsid_2645000/ 2645361.stm

Playing the advantage

The game should flow without too much interruption from the umpires. This means that, if they see an offence that is not creating a disadvantage for the non-offending team, or where stopping the game would cause a disadvantage to the non-offending side, they play the advantage. This means that the game is allowed to continue.

The umpire signalling for an advantage.

The umpires need to keep the game under control though and will stop the game if a player offends repeatedly, if the decision to play advantage would be unfair to the non-offending side and if playing the advantage would be a controversial decision.

Can you give me an example of the kind of offence where the umpire would play advantage?
If a single player is offside but does not have possession of the ball and is taking no active part in the game, the advantage will be played. It might be unfair to stop the game and give a free pass to the non-offending side from the place where the offending player was standing – especially if the other team already had possession of the ball.

Free passes

Free passes are used to redress many rule infringements and are used when the technical rules are broken. They are taken by a player from the non-offending team at the place where the offence occurred, or where the ball was when play was stopped.

Free passes are awarded when:

- late arrivals or substitutes come onto the court while the game is in progress, rather than waiting for a stoppage or for a goal to be scored

- a player catches or touches the ball from the centre pass, but is not inside the centre third
- a player is offside. This means that a player has moved into an area of the court that she is not designated to play in
- a player goes out of court for no clear reason, such as for taking a throw-in or collecting a ball
- a player hits the ball with her fist, falls on the ball to gain possession, or deliberately kicks the ball
- the player is not standing up but laying or kneeling on the ground, rather than standing upright to try and gain possession of the ball or to pass it
- a player uses the goalpost as a tool to lean on to regain the ball if it has gone out of court, or if she uses the post to keep her balance
- a player does not play the ball correctly (ie she bounces, drops or replays it, throws the ball and replays it before it has been touched by another player, or rolls it to another player)
- a player takes another shot at the goal, after it has missed but not rebounded from some part of the goalpost
- the pass is short (ie a third player cannot pass between the thrower and the receiver)
- the ball travels over an entire third without being touched or caught by another player
- the footwork rule is broken.

Remember that you cannot take a shot at the goal with a free pass.

Also remember that you still have to obey the rules when you're taking a free pass, so make sure you've taken the throw within three seconds and keep those feet under control!

Penalty passes

Penalty passes are awarded in the case of:

- obstruction (remember: being closer than 0.9 m (3 ft) to the player in possession of the ball is an obstruction)
- contact
- a player moving a goalpost.

> A player obstructs another player, makes contact or moves a goalpost. It is clearly unfair, and to play an advantage would be unfair to the non-offending team.

> The umpire blows her whistle and signals obstruction.

> The throw can be taken by any player on the non-offending team, as long as he is allowed in the third where the infringement occurred. The player who has been penalised must stand to one side and away from the player taking the throw, and must not take any active part in play until the thrower has thrown the ball.

> The player making the throw makes his pass within three seconds and obeys the footwork rule.

If an offence takes places in the goal circle and the non-offending team is in attack, they have the option of a penalty pass or shot. This means that the goal shooter or goal attack can either pass to another player or take a shot at the goal.

Player profile

As a successful international defender, Amanda Newton knows her netball. She has been part of the England squad since 1996, having previously played in the team that won the bronze medal in the under-21 World Youth Cup. She was also part of the teams that won bronze medals at the 1998 Commonwealth Games and the 1999 World Championships. By the 2003 World Netball Championships, Amanda had assumed the role of vice- captain of the squad, but then suffered a long-term injury. Happily for the England netball squad, and for Amanda, she has since recovered and is once again part of England's solid defence.

Throw-ins

Throw-ins are taken when the ball goes out of court. Remember, a ball is out of court only when it touches the ground, someone or something outside the goal or the side lines. As long as the ball is in the air, players can try to retrieve the ball by leaning over the line and either catching it or batting it back onto court.

The ball goes out of court.

↓

The umpire signals for a throw-in, which is taken at the point where the ball went out of court.

↓

The throw-in is given to the team that is not responsible for the ball being out of court. This means that, if the ball was thrown out of court, it will be the opposing teammate to the last player who touched the ball that takes the throw-in. If a player was out of court and had possession of the ball, it will be her opponent that takes the throw-in.

↓

All the players, apart from the one taking the throw-in, must be on court.

↓

The player taking the throw-in stands at the point where the ball went out of court. One or both feet must be behind the line. It is important not to come back onto the court until the ball has been thrown. It is also important for the player not to stray offside (ie stray along the outside of the court so that she is in line with a third in which she is not permitted to play).

↓

The ball is thrown. The player must remember the three-second and the footwork rules. It is also important to remember whereabouts on the court the ball can be thrown. If the player is standing on the goal line, the ball can only travel into that particular goal third, rather than covering the length of the court. However, if the throw-in is taken from the side line, the player taking the throw-in could throw the ball into the goal third or the centre third.

Toss-ups

As well as using the
toss-up to decide who
gets possession of the
ball if two players gain
possession at the same
time, the toss-up is also
used to decide possession where two
players from opposing teams have
simultaneously infringed the rules.

The umpire signals that a toss-up is
required.

The toss-up is taken at the point where
the offence occurred. Both players
must be able to play in the third where
the toss-up is to take place. If not, the
toss-up will take place in the centre
circle and will be taken by two players
designated to play in that zone. None
of the other players must be involved.

The two players face one another
towards their own attacking goal ends.
They must be 0.9 m (3 ft) apart from
leading foot to leading foot. It does not
matter how the two players stand, but
their arms and hands must be straight
down by their sides.

The umpire stands midway between
the two players. She holds the ball on
the palm of her hand just below the
shoulder level of the shortest player
(as if they were standing upright).

The umpire blows the whistle and
'flicks it vertically, not more than
600 mm (2 ft) in the air, as the whistle
is blown'[4].

One of the players will gain possession
of the ball.

[4] Official Netball Rules, page 54

What sort of rules can be simultaneously broken?

All of them! Where teams are
evenly matched, it is inevitable that players
are going to reach the ball at the same
time. It is also inevitable in such an
action-packed game that the umpires are
not always going to be able to see exactly
who was responsible for what. Examples
of simultaneous offences include knocking
the ball out of court, being offside,
touching the ball and making contact.

What happens if one of the players moves before the whistle is blown?

A free pass is awarded to the other player.

Warning players

Netball players are expected to behave
according to the spirit of the game.
Umpires apply the penalties to players
who break the rules and can also suspend
players if they repeatedly break the rules,
or behave in an unfair way. Normally, the
umpire will give players a warning before
suspending them.

Umpires also have the power to increase
the impact of a penalty due to the
inappropriate behaviour of the offending
player. This can be achieved by advancing
the penalty; the umpire can move the
penalty pass further up the court towards
the goal (ie advancing the players who
have been infringed against).

When are warnings given?

Players will be warned if they
make an inappropriate comment
or behave in a way that is not in
keeping with the spirit of the game. This
normally means that they have repeatedly
broken the rules or have behaved in a way
that could be described as rough or
dangerous.

Suspending players

If a player is suspended, he is required to leave the court for a length of time specified by the umpire. The player's team must compete with a man down until the suspended player is permitted to return to the match. This can only be done when a goal is scored.

> A player has repeatedly broken the obstruction rule, for example.

> The umpire signals for the timekeeper to stop the clock or 'hold time'.

> The umpire tells the player what his offence is and how long he has been suspended for. This should be in proportion to the offence. The player must leave the court and, if it is an NSL or international match, sit beside the reserve umpire.

> The umpire tells the timekeeper how long the player has been suspended for and then signals the restart of the clock and the match by blowing her whistle.

> The game continues. The offending player's team must play with only six players (assuming that they started with seven and that only one player has been suspended).

> The player is allowed to return to court after the period of his suspension (this is after the next goal has been scored or after the next interval). The player must return to his designated playing position from which he was suspended.

Can the team reallocate playing positions while the suspended player is off court?

If the suspended player is the centre, another player may take the role during the time of the suspension but, when the suspended player returns to court, the other player must go back to her previous position.

Is suspension the ultimate sanction?

No. Umpires can order a player off the court so that they take no further part in the match. A player will only be ordered off for very serious misconduct.

Summary

1 The netball rules are about respecting one another. As long as players respect one another and their spectators, there is little likelihood of anyone behaving unfairly.

2 Umpires use signals and their whistles to communicate with the players.

3 If players break the technical rules, a free pass is awarded. These rules relate to holding the ball for more than three seconds, footwork and the way in which the ball is controlled.

4 Players who infringe the obstruction, intimidation and moving the goalposts rules will have a penalty pass awarded against them.

5 If an offence takes place in the goal circle, players need to remember that they cannot shoot at the goal if it is a free pass. If the award is a penalty pass, they can shoot at the goal.

6 If the ball goes out of court, a throw-in is awarded to the team that did not have possession of the ball before it went out of court. Players taking the throw-in must be outside the court and parallel to their designated playing third, or they will be offside.

7 The toss-up takes place where there is a simultaneous offence, if two players from opposing teams gain possession of the ball at the same time, or where the umpires do not know who last had possession of the ball.

8 It is important for players involved in the toss-up to wait until the whistle is blown before moving, or a free pass will be awarded against them.

9 Umpires can warn, suspend and, ultimately, send players off who repeatedly offend or behave in an unsporting manner. Players sitting on the substitutes' bench must abide by the same rules, or they can also be penalised.

10 If a player is suspended or sent out of the game, the remaining team must continue to play with one person down. A substitute cannot be brought onto the court to continue the game in place of the suspended or dismissed player.

11 If the missing player is the centre, one of the players already on court can take on the role.

12 The spirit of the game is very important. Netball players are expected to play to the best of their ability and in a sporting way.

Player profile

As a goal attack and goal shooter, **Pamela Cookey** has had plenty of opportunity to develop her talents with the England under-21 squad and also with Team Bath Force. Since entering the international arena in 2004, she has taken part in several Test Series and the Melbourne Commonwealth Games.

Training

A i What is this signal for and when does the umpire use it?

B You are the umpire. Decide what you would award in each of these cases.

Offence	Umpire Decision/Award
A player has come into the centre third before the centre pass has been taken.	
The ball has gone out of court.	
The person taking the throw-in has her foot inside the court.	
A player is offside but she does not have the ball and is taking no active part in the game.	

C When you watch a netball match, note down the ways in which the players and the spectators show their appreciation of good playing.

D Watch a netball match. Make a note of the different penalties that are awarded. Can you explain why the umpires make each of their decisions?

Chapter 10
Finding Out More

If you want to find out more about getting involved in netball, why not join a team – it could be at school or at a local club. England Netball, Northern Ireland Netball, Netball Scotland and the Welsh Netball Association are committed to developing netball for young people. In England, for example, there are nine regional offices responsible for helping to support and develop the game of netball. Details of these regional offices can be found on the England Netball website.

 The England Netball website has lots of links that could help you find a club:
www.england-netball.co.uk/game/newsletter.cfm

If you are based in Scotland, please visit www.netballscotland.com/juniorclubs.aspx

The Welsh Netball Association provides information about netball clubs, the contact numbers for development officers, information about its summer schools, and even some top tips on how to start up your own club. Find out more at:
www.welshnetball.co.uk/welsh_netball_association/index.html

If you live in Northern Ireland, contact Netball Northern Ireland at:

Netball Office
House of Sport
Upper Malone Road
Belfast BT9 5LA
Tel: 028-9038 3806
Email: netballni@houseofsportni.net
Alternatively, visit
http://homepage.ntlworld.com/the.beehive/ClubDirectory/n_ireland.htm

How about becoming a coach or an umpire? England Netball has a programme that might be of interest to you. The Young Netball Organiser's Course is designed for people between the ages of 14 and 18. Take the opportunity to become involved in officiating!

Top tip: Enjoy yourself. Netball is about having fun, keeping fit, having respect for the game and learning new skills.

Glossary

Attacking team	The team with possession of the ball.
Attacking third	The goal third of the court where a team attacks their opponent's defenders, in order to attempt to shoot and score a goal.
Back line	The boundaries at the ends of the court.
Bounce pass	The ball is allowed to bounce when it is passed. Good technique is for the ball to bounce only once.
Centre circle	The circle in the middle of the court where play is started from and where play restarts after a goal has been scored.
Centre third	The middle third of the court.
Centre pass	A pass taken from the centre circle to start the game and also to restart it after a goal has been scored. Rule 12 of the netball rules explains the way in which a centre pass must be taken and the penalties for not taking or receiving a centre pass correctly.
Contact	Netball is a non-contact sport. This means that opponents must have no physical contact.
Defending team	The team that does not have possession of the ball.
Defending third	The goal third of the court where a team defends its goal from the opponents.
Dodging	Evading an opponent to create an opportunity to receive the ball.
Fake	Players pretend to pass in one direction but actually pass in another direction.
Feed	A pass into the shooting circle.
Feint	A move made by a player to get free from a defender, by pretending to go one way but then going in a different direction.
Footwork	A player catching the ball must keep the foot that touched the ground first, grounded. They may pivot on it to change direction. If the grounded foot is removed from the ground, the ball must be released before the foot makes contact with the ground again. If a player lands on both feet, it is up to the player to decide which foot is the grounded foot.
Getting free	Attacking players try to get themselves in a position where they are available to receive passes.
Goal circle	The semi-circle at either end of the court. The goal shooter (GS) and goal attack (GA) can only score goals by shooting from inside the semi-circle. It is also called the shooting circle.
Held ball	Players who receive the ball are allowed to keep it for only three seconds. If, after three seconds, a player has not passed the ball or taken a shot at the goal, she has committed an offence.

Landing foot   When a player catches the ball, he needs to abide by the footwork rule. This rule explains that the foot that touches the ground first is the landing foot. Players need to understand which their landing foot is, because the footwork rule is very specific about the kinds of movements that the player in possession of the ball can make.

Man-to-man   Each defender marks her opponent.

Marking   Players stay close to their opponents to prevent them from receiving passes.

Offside   A player moves outside the area she is allowed to play in. It does not matter if she has the ball or not.

Passing distance   A third player should be able to step between the player throwing the ball and the player catching the ball. This prevents unfair play, by simply giving the ball from one player to the next.

Pivot   A player pivots his foot on the ground to change direction, but does not lose contact with the ground.

Rebound   If the ball bounces off the goalpost after a missed shot, it is called a rebound. Players from both teams can compete for possession (of the ball) after a missed shot.

Replay   An illegal action whereby a player catches or touches the ball after passing it, before another player has caught/touched the ball.

Shooting circle   The semi-circle at either end of the court. The goal shooter (GS) and goal attack (GA) can only score goals by shooting from inside the semi-circle. It is also called the goal circle.

Thirds   The court is divided into thirds. The ball must not be thrown over a complete third, unless it is caught or touched by another member of the team other than the player throwing the ball. Teams may opt for zonal defence, whereby they share the responsibility of marking players inside the third where the ball is currently being played.

Throw-in   The method for returning the ball into play when it has left the court.

Transverse lines   The lines that divide the court into thirds.

Toss-up   If possession of the ball is undecided, for example, because two players from opposing teams have caught the ball together, the umpire will throw the ball up in the air between the two players involved to decide who will take possession.

Umpire   There are two umpires who control the game.

    Look here for a full list of netballing words:
www.nevisculturama.net/nevisnetball/glossary.htm

Answers

Chapter 5

B i and ii

Player	Full name of position	Defensive third	Centre third	Attacking third
GS	Goal shooter			✓
GA	Goal attack		✓	✓
WA	Wing attack		✓	✓
C	Centre	✓	✓	✓
WD	Wing defence	✓	✓	
GD	Goal defence	✓	✓	
GK	Goal keeper	✓		

iii GD and GK   iv GS and GA

Chapter 6

A i Shooting at the goal. ii She is in the goal third inside the goal circle. iii WA

B i False ii True iii True iv False v True

Chapter 7

A i Yes ii No

B i The umpire should award a penalty pass to the other team because the defending player is closer than 0.9 m (3 ft). ii No offence.

Chapter 8

i a. obstruction b. held ball c. offside d. contact (leg) e. footwork

ii Obstructing and contact would both result in a penalty pass or shot at goal.

Chapter 9

A Advantage. This is played from where the umpire feels that to stop the game would disadvantage the non-offending side.

B

Offence	Penalty
A player has come into the centre third before the centre pass has been taken.	A free pass to the opposing team to be taken from where the infringement occurred.
The ball has gone out of court.	Award a throw-in to the side that did not have possession of the ball.
The person taking the throw-in has their foot inside the court.	Award a free pass to the other team.
A player is offside but she does not have the ball and is taking no active part in the game.	Play advantage only if the opposing team is in possession of the ball. A free pass is awarded if the infringing player's team has possession of the ball.

Bibliography

All England Netball Association (2004) *Official Netball Rules*. Hertfordshire: All England Netball.

Blackall, Bernie (2000) *Top Sport: Netball*. Oxford: Heinemann. ISBN: 0-431085-14-5.

Crouch, Heather (2005) *Netball Coaching*. London: A & C Black. ISBN: 0-713673-29-X.

Galsworthy, Betty (1996) *The Skills of the Game – Netball*. Marlborough: The Crowwood Press. ISBN: 1-861260-04-0.

Shakespear, Wilma (1997) *Netball – Steps to Success*. Champaign, Illinois: Human Kinetics. ISBN: 0-873229-84-3.

Useful websites

http://en.wikipedia.org/wiki/Netball

www.bbc.co.uk

www.netballfun.com

www.netballonline.com

www.ucl.ac.uk/~uczcw11/netball.htm

Index